Ruby's Secret

Written by Rosalind Malam
Illustrated by Jennifer Cooper

Last summer, I went to live with Dad. My old dog Skipper came, too. But, soon after that, Skipper died. He'd been my friend as long as I could remember, and I was sure I'd never love another dog.

One day, I was in the garden when I saw a strange dog.

"Hey, Dad!" I yelled. "There's a dog in our garden!"

Dad came to look. The dog had white socks and a short tail that nearly wagged itself right off when she saw us.

"Where did she come from?" asked Dad. "Put Skipper's lead on her. We have to find out where she belongs."

We asked everywhere, but no one owned the dog. No one had even seen her before.

"Good," I said. "We can keep her! Let's call her Ruby."

"I'm sure the dog has a name of her own," said Dad. "And I'm sure she does have owners and that they'll be missing her."

Ruby crept up to the table and looked at my plate. "The only thing **she's** missing right now is dinner!" I said, laughing.

We put advertisements in the paper, but nobody answered them. Ruby stuck to me like bubblegum. We played games and went exploring together. Ruby loved the beach more than anything.

She always knew how to get our attention. When Nana came to visit, Ruby charged around the room with a pair of Dad's underpants! She just knew Nana didn't like dogs inside.

If we worked outside, there was Ruby, poking her nose into everything. Once she pounced on a rose bush Dad was about to plant . . . then, before you could say "jumping jellybeans", she'd run off with the hose!

One day, Dad noticed that Ruby was looking fatter. "You've been giving her too much junk food," he told me.

But I'd noticed something, too — how often Ruby sat staring out the window, as if she was waiting for someone.

I didn't want to think about it.

Over the holidays, Dad said we could visit Aunt Rosie. It took four hours to get there, so we left home early. We were almost there when Dad asked if I'd remembered to pack Ruby's food. I hadn't, so we stopped at a pet shop.

It was Dad who saw the photo stuck to the pet shop window. It was a photo of a dog with white socks. It was definitely Ruby. Under the photo, in big red letters, the notice said:

MISSING, ALLIE

And there was a phone number.

I just couldn't stop crying. I begged Dad not to make the phone call. He hugged me tight and said, "Remember when you first came to stay with me, and Skipper disappeared? And how you felt when he was returned the next day?"

I remembered . . . there are some things you never forget!

It was the hardest thing I'd ever done, letting Ruby go home. When Dad took her back, he wanted me to come, too. I couldn't do it. Ruby put her chin on my shoulder as I whispered goodbye. She couldn't understand why I was so sad.

How Ruby came to us will always be a mystery, but time really dragged when she left us.

Then, one night, the telephone rang.
Dad went to answer it and came back
looking excited.

"That was Jack, Ruby's owner. He wants us
to visit and says he has a surprise for you,"
he said.

"Is he giving Ruby back to me?"

Dad looked at me sadly. "No. Ruby's back
where she belongs. But she'd love to see
you again. Are you ready to see her, too?"

**Of course I wanted to see Ruby, but it
would make me sad all over again.**

Dad put his arm around me. "Perhaps it's
time to get another dog — one of your
very own."

"Have another dog? After Ruby? Never!"

13

Dad smiled. He'd heard those words before. "Did loving Ruby make you love Skipper less?" he asked.

I thought about it. Loving Ruby hadn't changed the way I felt about Skipper. He has a special place in my heart that no one else could fill. But Ruby has her special place, too, and nothing will ever take that away.

So Dad and I went to Jack's place. Jack seemed really happy to see me.

"I can't thank you enough for looking after my dog," he said. "It was lonely without her. Your dad thought that junk food had made her fat, but . . . follow me!"

He led us around the back of his house to a shed.

There was Ruby, lying inside a large
wooden box. She wagged her short
tail and whined. She seemed happy to see
me, but she didn't get up. I could hardly
believe my eyes when I saw the reason
why! Three little puppies were snuggled
beside her, fast asleep.

"That little red one looks like her mother,"
Jack was saying. "But the striped
one — he's a real clown! Take your pick."

So everything turned out well in the end.
I had my very own puppy. We love each
other, and he comes with me everywhere.
And every holiday we all go back to see
Jack and Ruby.

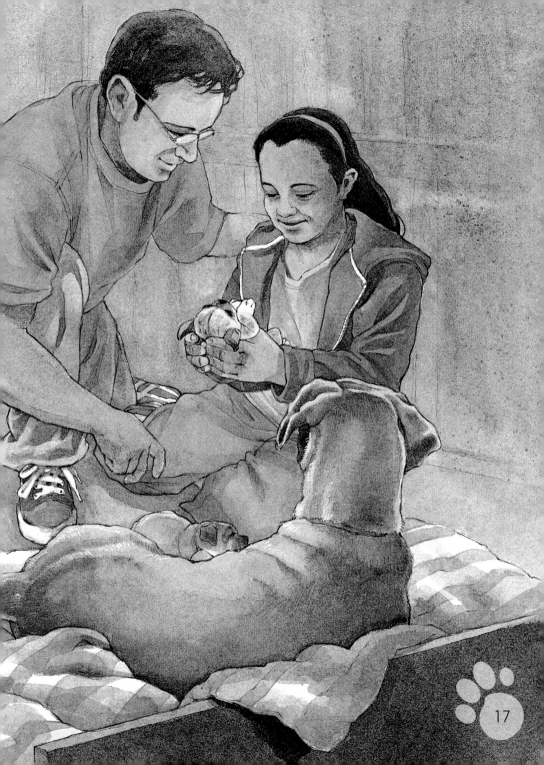

Ruby's Secret is a Recount.

A **recount** tells . . .

- **who** the story is about (the characters)
- **when** the story happened
- **where** the story is set.

Who	When	Where
	last summer	

A recount tells what happens.

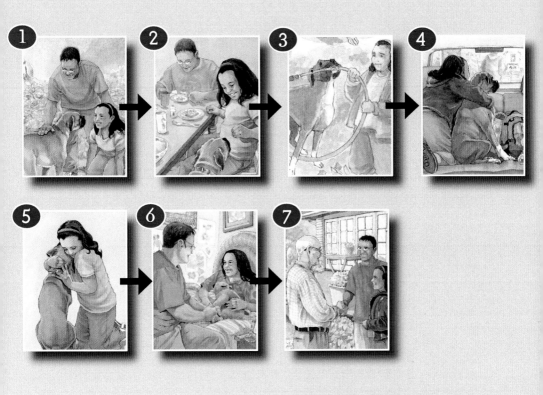

A recount has a **conclusion**.

19

■■■■ Guide Notes

Title: Ruby's Secret
Stage: Fluency

Text Form: Recount
Approach: Guided Reading
Processes: Thinking Critically, Exploring Language, Processing Information
Written and Visual Focus: Text Highlights

THINKING CRITICALLY
(sample questions)
- What do you think this story could be about? Look at the title and discuss.
- Look at the cover. How do you know that the girl and her father like animals?
- Look at pages 2 and 3. What sort of person do you think the narrator is? Why do you think that?
- Look at pages 4 and 5. What do you think the narrator and her dad did to try and find Ruby's owner?
- Look at pages 10 and 11. How do you think Ruby's owner felt when he heard that she had been found?
- Look at pages 12 and 13. Why do you think the narrator said that seeing Ruby would *make me sad all over again*?

EXPLORING LANGUAGE

Terminology
Spread, author and illustrator credits, imprint information, ISBN number

Vocabulary
Clarify: charged, whined, crept, exploring, pounced, definitely, shoulder, believe
Adjectives: *white* socks, *junk* food, *big red* letters
Pronouns: I, he, she, her, us
Simile: Ruby stuck to me *like bubblegum*
Focus the students' attention on **homonyms**, **antonyms** and **synonyms** if appropriate.

Print Conventions
Apostrophes – possessive (Ruby's Secret, Skipper's lead), ellipses, dashes, colon